Hide and Seek

Find the Fish

By Cate Foley

Children's Press
A Division of Grolier Publishing
New York / London / Hong Kong / Sydney
Danbury, Connecticut

Photo Credits: Cover, © Fleetham/Animals Animals; pp. 5, 6, 7, 21 © Index Stock Photgraphy Inc.; pp. 9, 10, 11, 21 © Zig Leszcznski/Animals Animals; pp. 13, 14, 15, 21 © Clay Wiseman/ Animals Animals; pp. 17, 18, 19, 21 © Fleetham/Animals Animals

Contributing Editor: Jennifer Ceaser
Book Design: Nelson Sa

Visit Children's Press on the Internet at:
http://publishing.grolier.com

Library of Congress Cataloging-in-Publication Data

Foley, Cate.
    Find the fish / by Cate Foley.
      p. cm. — (Hide and seek)
    Summary: Simple text and photographs challenge the reader to find hidden fish in their natural
      environments.
    ISBN 0-516-23095-6 (lib. bdg.) — ISBN 0-516-23020-4 (pbk.)
    1. Fishes—Juvenile literature. 2. Camouflage (Biology)—Juvenile literature. [1. Fishes.
    2. Camouflage (Biology) 3. Picture puzzles.] I. Title.

QL617.2.F65 2000
597—dc21

J597 (READER)
FOL
270- 2945

00-024626

Contents

1 A Long, Thin Fish   6

2 A Flat Fish   10

3 A Fish with Spots   14

4 A Spiky Fish   18

5 New Words   22

6 To Find Out More   23

7 Index   24

8 About the Author   24

Look closely.

Can you see the **gap** in the rocks?

A fish is hiding there.

This fish is an eel.

It is long and thin like a snake.

It hides between rocks.

Look closely.

Can you see the bottom of the ocean?

A fish is living down there.

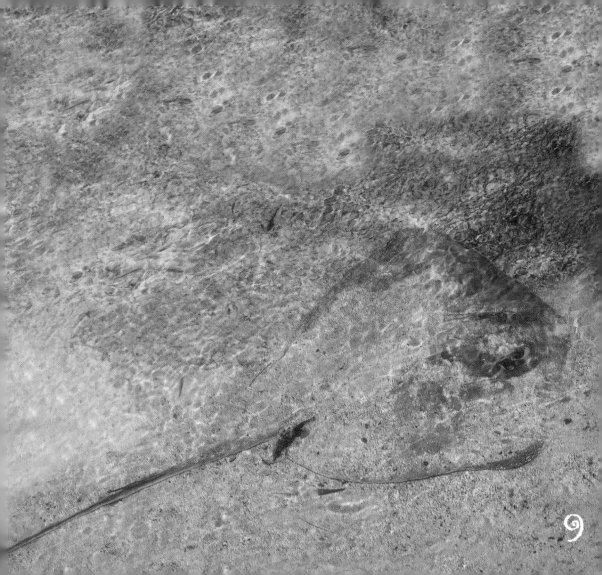

The ray is a **flat** fish.

It goes under the sand to hide.

11

Look closely.

Can you see spots behind the rocks?

A fish is **floating** there.

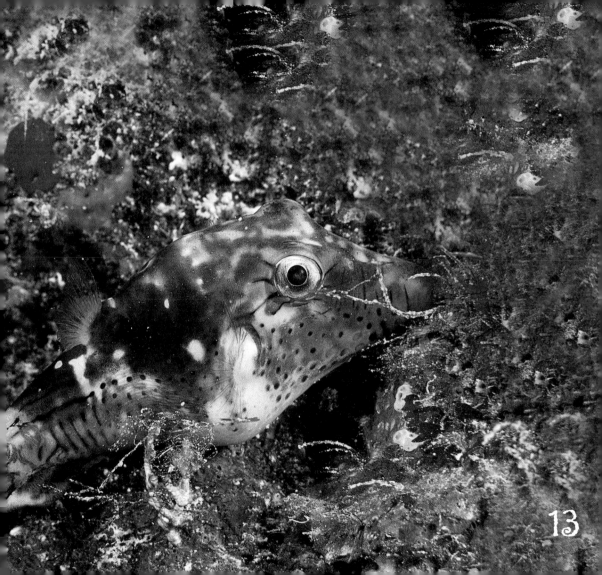

13

This is a puffer fish.

It has spots to help it blend in with the rocks.

14

15

Look closely.

Can you see the rocks?

A fish is resting there.

17

This is the scorpion fish.

It looks like a **spiky** stone.

It changes its color to blend in with different rocks.

Which fish would you like to meet in the sea?

20

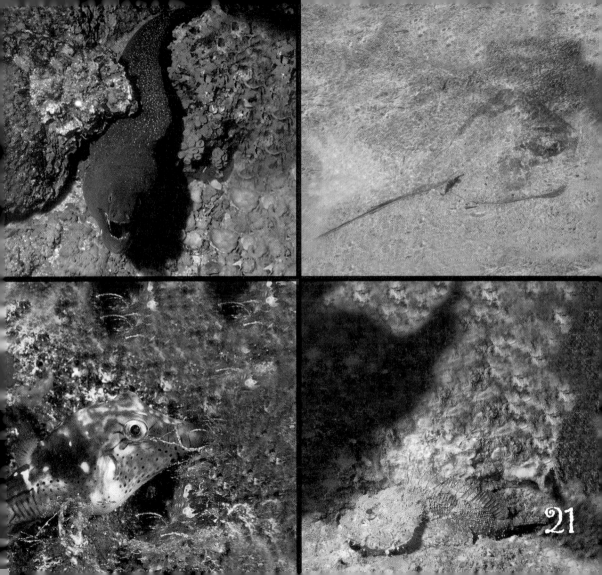

21

New Words

flat (**flat**) not thick

floating (**floht**-ing) resting
or moving slowly in water

gap (**gap**) a crack or hole

spiky (**spi**-kee) sharp and
pointed

To Find Out More

Books
Hello Fish!: Visiting the Coral Reef
by Sylvia A. Earle and Wolcott Henry
National Geographic Society

Searchin' Safari: Looking for Camouflaged Creatures
by Jeff O'Hare and Marc Nadel
Boyds Mill Press

Web Sites
Fish FAQ
http://www.wh.whoi.edu/faq/index.html
The Northeast Fisheries Science Center answers your questions
about fish. There are lots of fish pictures and cool fish facts.

Ask Shamu
http://www.seaworld.org/ask_shamu/asindex.html
Here are answers to a lot of questions about fish and
other sea animals.

23

Index

eel, 6

flat, 10
floating, 12

gap, 4

puffer fish, 14

ray, 10
rocks, 4, 6, 12,
    14, 16, 18

sand, 10
scorpion fish, 18
spiky, 18

About the Author
Cate Foley writes and edits books for children. She lives in New Jersey with her husband and son.

Reading Consultants
Kris Flynn, Coordinator, Small School District Literacy, The San Diego County Office of Education

Shelly Forys, Certified Reading Recovery Specialist, W.J. Zahnow Elementary School, Waterloo, IL

Peggy McNamara, Professor, Bank Street College of Education, Reading and Literacy Program